Into a Salt Marsh Heart

poems by

Marie-Louise Eyres

Finishing Line Press
Georgetown, Kentucky

Into a Salt Marsh Heart

ACKNOWLEDGMENTS

St. Catherine's Hill—Highly Commended & published in the *Ginkgo AONB Prize*, 2020
Sky Dance—first published in *ffraid* magazine, 2021
Along Bayswater Road—first published by *Agenda*, 2020
Inside Scorton North Yorks—first published by *Ink, Sweat & Tears*, 2020
In Spirit Only—Shortlisted in the *Bridport Prize* 2018
Home—first published by *Broken Spine*, 2022
Limbs and Leaves—first published by *Ink, Sweat & Tears*, 2019
Last photo of Dad—first published by *The Poet's Republic*, 2022

Publisher: Leah Huete de Maines
Editor: Christen Kincaid
Cover Art: Thomas Eakins, 1874, title Sketch of Max Schmitt in a Single Scull
Author Photo: Marie-Louise Eyres
Cover Design: Elizabeth Maines McCleavy

Order online: www.finishinglinepress.com
also available on amazon.com

Author inquiries and mail orders:
Finishing Line Press
PO Box 1626
Georgetown, Kentucky 40324
USA

Table of Contents

St Catherine's Hill, Winchester

A mound, I'm shaped
with a perpetual, expectant hump.
A scheduled, ancient monument,

beneath my copse I'm solid,
chalked-in deep, white as morning milk,
but marbled through with fecund earth.

On spring and summer days,
I wear my fanciest of grasses,
my Cocksfoot, my Timothy,

my Crested Dogstails,
all purple tipped and breeze-swept,
like the fringes of a shawl.

With Whitethroat and Linnet's song,
I coax straggling ramblers out
of The Black Bottle, away

from clinking, yeasty pints and onto paths
bedded-in between the fresh,
weed-strewn river-slits

of these ancient meadows,
plague pits, ditch and bank.
My verdurous under-water vines

are live with speckled-brown trout,
vole and elusive otter. Walkers may
follow these shallow streams

all the way to my turf-carved druid maze.
The Celtic tools are long gone,
footprints too—but beside the beech trees,

with their partial shade
you'll find some horizontal, fallen boughs
the most natural, recurring human seats.

And with all the souls who passed through in earlier times,
we'll share the quiet, the cool, the mauve-lit
end of days.

Sky Dance

We travel to the coast for a week in Summer,
I stay in the motel bed, run air-con against the heat,
hide from fried food, a lack of vegetables in town.

Then one dusk, the night before we leave,
we drive out to see wild horses—
pale dapples, browns, stallions in the distance,

the edge of their world more than a grassy bank,
a silt channel that sends black ducks,
clapper rails and snow geese,

even yellow-crested night herons in all their fancy pomp,
along sluice streams until they raise their wings
to join the clouds.

Branches of bald cypress, holly, chestnut,
are flung wide towards the sky,
as if in celebration of this flight,

while their long, tangled roots sink like arteries
below the mirror of sea into the mud flats,
into a salt marsh heart.

Along Bayswater Road

It snows heavily at three o'clock,
so leaving work at six, I walk a wordless hour
from Soho office to flat in Holland Park,
forfeiting the slow ride on the 94,
the soggy coat-wrestlers on the tube.

I make fresh tracks, black boots
across white snow—I fancy myself
as a gazelle when I quickly pass
the heat of traffic, the collective fug
of engines slowed.

Next summer, this becomes a balmy stroll,
that unpicks the stitch of a long day,
but on 7/7 I meet my fella early, halfway home,
both of us unsure what qualifies as safe,
beyond the ordered, open space
around the Serpentine.

In August, from the bus I spot my father dashing
through Hyde Park on his daily ten-mile run,
dripping sweat from face to foot,
he doesn't know I'm here of course—
when he turns his bony back on me
at the rib-like curve of Carriage Drive.

He's sixty now, heading straight past the memorials
that lead to Albert Hall,
and I want to get off this bus,
catch up with him—
but as always, he is just too far ahead.

Inside, Scorton, North Yorkshire

After lunch she whispers
to the carved mahogany table legs
feels around for the mouse
cut into the back of the armchair
where her grandmother
reads paperback mysteries.
She names that mouse Moses.
Then she slides away
from the snoring chorus of adults,
the ashtrays, where forgotten
after-lunch smokes still burn
and drift their bitter incense.
The coal-shed's black hills
are piled up, photonegatives
of snowdrifts against dusty walls,
and here she hopes for a long life
of blue flame for each waiting carbon stone.
The pantry's a cool sacristy, full of
edible icons, a yeasty bread-tin,
jam jars in shades of oranges and plums,
homemade beer in plastic vats
with mustard stains. She incants
their names, blessing the contents
of each greasy tub
and honeyed pot in turn.

Outside, Scorton, North Yorkshire

She's outside in the day
just before it shifts to dusk,
in time to see next door's
thread of woodsmoke drifting
from the roof into the flat,
woven clouds. A single airplane
unstitches this vast blanket
of vaporous weave and in vain,
she wishes it whole again.
The loose cobbled path
at the back of the old house
leads to dry stone walls,
and if she climbs, she spies
a gap, the neighbour taking down
dark work-shirts, wooden pegs,
a son steadying the plough-horse
back to stable, leaving deep grooves
in mud like crescent moons.
They don't notice as she brushes
her lips across the wall's broom-moss,
whispering to any spirits
who may be resting there.
Between the outside
and the inside is a greenhouse
paved with oxblood tiles.
She stops to close her eyes,
inhales the heady fumes of fresh,
wax-polished floors, faint scents
of dried earth, in long neglected seedling pots.
These elements cast their pungent
spells as she sits quite still
on dark red steps.

Soft Landing

Black-currant juice sprays
up the woodchip walls,
as she trips
down the stairs.

Some days she slips
on the dark parquet floors,
their polish a cool relief
against her hot face.

Other times she lands
near the porcelain curve
of the bowl where they
flushed the belly-up fish.

Just the once she collapses
inside a wardrobe in half-light,
where she's glad for the moon dust,
among soft-leather shoes.

Years later she feels
she just stepped off a fair ride,
all balance upended
by the speed of the tracks.

She'll stagger and sway
one step to the right,
how a radio can hold you
a moment, with song.

Now synapses spin
in her head every night,
they reverb and echo
each hard, back-handed blow.

Walking up Church Lane, West Wycombe

The old village prison's here, six feet by three,
with fat brown lice who tuck inside the wooden walls
that feed and shade them from the drying sun.

This path gets steep, we pass the row of cottages,
green paint, red brick and flower baskets,
all with the faintest streak of traffic soot.

Darker routes through woods
lead to golden barleycorn and signs for trails,
that earn the local Scouts bright badges on their sleeves.

And looming at the peak, is grey-speckled St. Lawrence,
guarded close by foliage—the yew trees shield us
from the heat, transform our faded state.

The grass is carpet-short where ramblers tread
on longer walks and it's here we often choose to sit,
looking out across the hill towards the chalky caves.

It's England of course so the summer breeze
turns cool and my daughter who runs through
longer purple grass must pull her jacket close.

Oh Dad, if you could only see the rubbish
that has blown along from cars when people parked
outside the church to snack, discarding all their plastics to the wind.

But your strong bones are now wrapped in linen gauze,
boxed deep in burial grounds just visible
from this same vantage point.

I hope the hawthorn and dry-stone walls buffer you
from the busy road, the butchers, the pubs,
the trucks that rattle like devils through the night.

They used to shake your roof then you, awake.

Inventory: Items left by my father

Bedroom: one unmade bed,
a discarded pillow,

steel-rimmed glasses propped
on an open book.

Bathroom: two-tone shaving brush,
bone-dry pot of shaving soap.

Kitchen: one blue and white apron,
flour handprints,

shelves of raisins, demerara, walnuts,
rolled into bags, elasticated shut.

One freshly baked pie on a rack,
the scent of chicken,

a radio switched off,
one stained teapot,

an old scouring brush,
one cloth, still damp over a single tap.

Dining room: one empty table,
running shoes kicked off beneath.

Pantry: this week's crop of butternut squash,
a gigantic pair of green, rubber boots.

Bedroom: one unmade bed,
a discarded pillow,

steel-rimmed glasses propped
on an open book.

In Spirit Only

My dad is here, just a few steps behind me,
catching up fast with the stride of his enormous feet.

I hear him pant and shoe leather sighs as it twists
when we turn the corner of Durbin Lane on this brisk walk.

I could never keep up with him before,
running three quick steps to keep up with his one,

but now he is three steps behind,
his head brushes the low hanging leaves like a breeze—

He was by the stairs in the night when I took my daughter
down to the kitchen to get warm milk,

he whispered a breath and the carpeted stair creaked.
He didn't tell me how to wash up the pans,

or be careful of waking my mother with clatter,
he was quiet.

And out walking today, I keep turning round just in case,
just in case I can catch sight of him.

Home

It was leaving the farm
in the rain
I remember the most,

not the glow of sunset across metal roofs,
making magenta
at day's end,

but the silence of empty silos.

Barn windows held
no reflections from
sunnier days,

gone was the thin scent of sourdough.

Dirt worked its way
into wood
where paint had cracked,

deep as layers of skin.

Prints in the mud from boots,
and the half-lame dog
who never left his side,

all washed away.

Early Retirement

There's a photo of my gran, a polaroid
turned sallow decades on. She's standing by a window,
gazing out towards the afternoon, her arms
are crossed, as if holding back a sigh.

She's looking at the plant that drapes
it's purple flowers round the window-frame,
and up the wall outside.

Her first year here, the crab-apple bloomed,
weighed down with red and yellow globes,
like Christmas at Fortnum's.

So, she had a go at jamming, big stainless pots,
long-hoarded bags of sugar put to use.
It took a week.

Glass jars filled up, ginger or rosemary,
with crab-apple in jellied shades of gold.
They cooled on shelves around the house.

A year later, all the fruit fell,
and rotted into grass, sour gobstoppers
left for badgers and blackbirds.

And in this faded picture, looking out that window,
I know she is thinking, *How can I get rid
of that blasted weed?*

I know because the next time we visit,
I go to fill the kettle and the wisteria
has vanished.

My mum, quietly asks what happened,
Oh it died, Gran says, *it had to go.*
And she waves the lie away, into the steam
rising from her tea.

Limbs and Leaves

Escaping the dry heat of the house,
we step into the mild, Boxing Day damp.
Our noses fill with the sweet stench
of silage and fallen fruits at the end of the garden.

Lying beneath bare trees,
a brightly coloured apple blanket
unraked after the Autumn storm,
rots by design, into the soil.

We stroll past the old piggery full of pruned back roses,
the cowsheds crammed with firewood,
too heavy to lug into the house this year,
too dusty for our eyes.

The greenhouse shelters a forest of geraniums
bowing to greet us, limbs and leaves gather mildew.
Under these windows angled to the sky,
rumours the scent of decay.

Last Photo of Dad

He's front seat in a double scull, the spoons
of blades submerged, strong legs, knees bent, chin up.
The looms of oars point back like wings
about to launch. This late June sky is overcast,
he grips the oars, with steely upward glance,
that says *I must push on.* The faulty wiring
of his heart's already tripped, he'd fallen
on a run, then bled against the asphalt
in the dark. He capsized weeks before
this photograph was shot, laughed off the murky
chill of River Thames. On Sunday he's forecast
to row but dies instead, with fleeting thoughts
of what, we wonder—copper beeches,
muddy riverbank, perhaps us cheering on.

Basil Fawlty as Conduit

We were watching Fawlty Towers
last summer during lockdown,
it was the episode when Manuel
lost his rat.

About halfway through, the punchline
lands when Manuel's scrabbling
on his knees inside a mucky shed,
whispering, *Basil, Basil?*

My son Tom, burst out with
Oh, he named the rat after Basil!
then half fell off the sofa laughing,
as he lost control of arms and legs.

And suddenly I remembered
watching this episode the first time,
in the late 70s with my dad,
one winter evening before a power-cut.

Dad had howled in glee
just the same way, with all the flailing
of his limbs off the sofa,
inside our Essex house.

Sometimes I hear dad whistling
in our kitchen, though he isn't here.
He used to do it while shelling peas
for lunch or folding laundry for mum.

I hear it these days, equally as tuneless,
while my son waits for his videogames
to load. It's my old dad's way of saying,
despite his absence, *Hello, darling girl.*

Marie-Louise Eyres started her career in theatre in the UK and Germany. She became a writing agent in London, where she managed a successful stable of TV, film and theatre writers until moving to the USA with her family. She received her MFA in 2020 from Manchester Writing School, after a brain tumor diagnosis in 2018.

She has been highly commended and a finalist in many poetry prizes and in 2021, was a winner in Poetry News' "Lesser Loss" competition. Her work can be found in poetry journals in the US, UK and Ireland, including *Stand, Acumen, Agenda, Portland Review, Poetry Magazine, Modern Poetry in Translation,* as well as the Bridport, Bedford, Live Canon and Ginkgo AONB prize anthologies.

Her micro, *When We Lived* in Los Angeles was published in 2021 by Alien Buddha Press and is available on Amazon. Her second micro, *Wolf Encounters,* was published in 2022, by Maverick Duck Press and is available as a free download. Marie-Louise is a naturalized US citizen who has lived mostly in New York, Washington DC and Los Angeles.